DEVOTIONAL

31 Devotionals to Comfort, Encourage, and Bring Peace in Christ

Luis Ranzolin

Copyright © 2015 Luis Ranzolin.

Legal Notice:

All rights reserved. No part of this book may be reproduced or transmitted in any form or by any means, electronic or mechanical, including photocopying, recording, or by any information storage and retrieval system without the written permission of the author and publisher, except where permitted by law. Reviewers may quote brief passages in their review.

Disclaimer:

This material is intended as general information only. No warranties or guarantees of any kind are expressed or implied by the author or publisher. Every effort has been made to provide accurate and complete information. By reading this material, the reader agrees the author and publisher are not responsible for any loss incurred resulting from the information contained in this publication. The reader is responsible for his or her own decisions and actions.

Scripture quotations are from the King James Version of the Bible.

Quotes that are underlined or in bold reflect emphasis added by author.

ISBN-13: 978-1523925964

ISBN-10: 1523925965

Dedication

This book is dedicated to the Father of our Lord Jesus Christ, the Father of mercies, and the God of all comfort; who comforteth us in all our tribulation, that we may be able to comfort them which are in any trouble, by the comfort wherewith we ourselves are comforted of God (2 Corinthians 1:3-4). Now unto the King eternal, immortal, invisible, the only wise God, be honour and glory for ever and ever. Amen (1 Timothy 1:17).

Table of Contents

1. All Things Work For Good 1
2. The Right Hand Of God 3
3. I Will Never Leave You 5
4. God Goes Before You 7
5. Joy Over You 9
6. Enemies At Peace 11
7. Prince Of Peace 13
8. Exceeding Your Expectations 15
9. Peace With God 17
10. Peaceable Habitations 19
11. Via Dolorosa 21
12. Peace, Be Still 23
13. Perfect Peace 25
14. Grace And Peace 27
15. Fruits Of The Spirit 29
16. I Will 31
17. Finding Rest 33
18. Freedom From Fear 35
19. Thoughts Of Peace 37
20. I Can Do All Things 39
21. Wait On The Lord 41
22. Wonderfully Made 43
23. Is Anything Too Hard For Me? 45

24. Peacemakers 47
25. Prayer That Avails Much 49
26. I Have Loved You 51
27. Preserve Your Soul 53
28. All Needs Supplied 55
29. The Comforter 57
30. God Of All Comfort 59
31. All Things New 61

One

ALL THINGS WORK FOR GOOD

And we know that all things work together for good to them that love God, to them who are the called according to His purpose (Romans 8:28).

This is one of the greatest promises in the entire word of God. Yet there are trials that are so hard to bear it defies belief that anything good can come out of them.

About three years ago my son got cancer. He was only five years old when we got the heartbreaking news. He almost died, but by the grace of God is doing fine now. I spoke with him just the other day about this promise. We are both baffled over how God will someday make that terrible ordeal work together for good.

Maybe that is where you are. You might be going through something even worse, and you might be wondering, "how can God make this work together for good?" Have faith. Every word of God proves true. Give Him a chance and He will make good on His promise.

I've had terrible things happen to me in the past that I can now see worked for the good. I remember one in particular. My entire being recoiled in horror at the thought that anything good could come out of it. The very idea seemed outrageous to me. And yet many years later I can testify that God did fulfill His word. Faithful is He who has promised (Hebrews 10:23).

The problem here is that we are finite. We can't see the end from the beginning, so we must learn to trust God. He is well acquainted with the future and knows that what appears to be right for us, will in the end not lead to our happiness. We need to be patient and let God work things out in His own time and way.

So friend, have faith in God, rest in His promises, and give Him a chance to surprise you; but recognize it might take some time. In the meantime, hang in there. God is with you and is concerned over what you are going through. Abide in Him and let Him comfort you. Like any nurturing parent with a hurting child, He desperately wants to take you into His arms and give you peace.

Two

THE RIGHT HAND OF GOD

Fear thou not; for I am with thee: be not dismayed; for I am thy God: I will strengthen thee; yea, I will help thee; yea, I will uphold thee with the right hand of My righteousness (Isaiah 41:10).

The Bible tells us that at the right hand of God are "pleasures for evermore" (Psalms 16:11). This pleasure the Psalmist is referring to is Jesus. It is He that is seated at the right hand of God (Mark 16:19). It is He that is the joy of every Christian. It is He that holds us up. And as Peter learned on that stormy night on the lake, it is He that hears us when we cry out, "Lord, save me."

And Peter answered Him and said, Lord, if it be Thou, bid me come unto Thee on the water.

And He said, Come. And when Peter was come down out of the ship, he walked on the water, to go to Jesus.

But when he saw the wind boisterous, he was afraid; and beginning to sink, he cried, saying, Lord, save me.

And <u>immediately Jesus stretched forth His hand, and caught him</u>, and said unto him, O thou of little faith, wherefore didst thou doubt? (Matthew 14:28-31).

Did you notice how close Jesus was when Peter got himself into trouble? Notice also that Peter cried out when he *began* to sink. This shows that in spite of his doubting, God prevented him from sinking quickly below the water. We know that is so because Peter had time to cry out, "Lord, save me" and Jesus was able to immediately catch him with His hand.

This event reminds me of a father teaching his little child how to swim in a children's swimming pool. It might be a little scary for the child, but the father is in control and is holding the child up with his hands. That lake was God's little swimming pool. Everything was under control. God tried to teach one of His little children how to walk on water. When the effort failed, God held up His child. Peter was never in any danger.

> *When thou passest through the waters, I will be with thee; and through the rivers, they shall not overflow thee (Isaiah 43:2).*

The experience of Peter shows us that we are walking on water when we walk in faith. The Bible says someday all of God's people shall stand on the sea of glass (Revelation 15:2). Only the faithful will be there. On that day, no one will sink. The storms of life will be over. The sea will be calm. And He who is seated at the right hand of God will hold His people up.

Like Peter, the Lord asks you to come to Him on the water. Will you make the decision today to trust Him fully and walk by faith and not by sight?

> *Though I walk in the midst of trouble, Thou wilt revive me: Thou shalt stretch forth thine hand... and Thy right hand shall save me (Psalms 138:7).*

Three

I Will Never Leave You

I will never leave thee, nor forsake thee (Hebrews 13:5).

God loves you with an everlasting love. You are one of His dear children. Those of us who are privileged to be parents have a wonderful window into the heart and mind of God.

For those who are not parents, have you noticed when you walk into the house of parents or grandparents with young children you see all those scribbles and drawings all over the place? Let me assure you as a parent, those are *masterpieces* you see on the walls! They are priceless. I also keep my little boy's precious notes to me tucked away in the drawer of my nightstand.

It's like that with God. Because of His love for you, everything you say and do is fascinating to Him. The Psalmist says:

What is man, that Thou art mindful of him (Psalms 8:4)?

God is very mindful of you. He is deeply interested and concerned with every aspect of your life. Your prayers to Him are stored in a vial (Revelation 5:8). That's God's "nightstand." Your good works are like those beautiful drawings you see on the walls of homes with small children. They are priceless to Him.

Can a woman forget her sucking child, that she should not have compassion on the son of her womb? yea, they may forget, yet will I not

> *forget thee. Behold, I have graven thee upon the palms of My hands; thy walls are continually before Me (Isaiah 49:15-16).*

Because of the taint of sin a human parent may lose compassion for their child, but not so with God. He knows the end from the beginning. He knows the fruits of sin and cannot be tempted with evil. He is pure and holy and always will be. His love for us is perfect. It is so deep, He has "graven" us on the palms of His hands. Christ's sacrifice on the cross is our eternal assurance of His unfailing love for us.

> *And in the wilderness, where thou hast seen how that the Lord thy God bare thee, as a man doth bear his son, in all the way that ye went, until ye came into this place (Deuteronomy 1:31).*

God will also "bare" us in love, just as he did Peter after he took his first few "baby steps" out on the water. So today, if your faith is weak and failing, remember that God is with you. Reach out to Him in faith.

> *Cast thy burden upon the Lord, and He shall sustain thee: He shall never suffer the righteous to be moved (Psalms 55:22).*

Four

God Goes Before You

And the Lord, He it is that doth go before thee; He will be with thee, He will not fail thee, neither forsake thee: fear not, neither be dismayed (Deuteronomy 31:8).

Rest assured, no matter where you go today, no matter what happens, God is already there. "He it is that doth go *before* thee." This is your assurance that when trouble arrives, God is not only with you, He is in front of you. That means He was already there when trouble struck. Follow Him and you will be safe. He has promised to not fail you, nor forsake you.

This is the same God that brought His people out of Egypt with great plagues against their enemies; parted the sea; sheltered His people in a pillar of cloud from the sun by day; gave them warmth in the desert with a pillar of fire by night; fed them with manna; and gave them water from the rock.

This is the same God that fulfilled His word when He brought the people of Israel into the promised land. It is this God that is with you today. His power has not diminished over time, neither has His compassion been in the least bit exhausted.

During His ministry, there are several instances where Jesus said, "follow me." When Jesus told the people of Israel, "before Abraham was, I AM" (John 8:58), He made it clear to them it was He that met with Moses at the burning bush. This means it was Jesus that led His people out of Egypt. And it is still He, the great I AM that goes before His people.

*And when He had called the people unto Him with His disciples also, He said unto them, Whosoever will <u>come</u> **after** <u>Me</u>, let him deny himself, and take up his cross, and **follow** <u>Me</u> (Mark 8:34).*

That means this business of denying ourselves and taking up our cross and *following* Him is the modern day equivalent of the wilderness wanderings of the people of Israel. So if you want to know what modern day cross bearing is all about, just read about the experiences the people of Israel had to go through on their way to the promised land. Let me assure you, the journey was not an easy one.

The soul of the people was much discouraged because of the way (Numbers 21:4).

Next time you get discouraged, remember, you are not the first one who took up cross bearing. The people of Israel took it up; Jesus took it up; and if you and I want to wind up in the same place where Moses and Jesus are, we need to take it up as well. Moses had some rough days, and Jesus even more so, but, in the end, they emerged victorious, and we can too. All we need to do is follow where Jesus leads.

If you study the experience of the people of Israel, you will see what made their journey so difficult was their lack of faith. God always took care of them, and yet they remained faithless and unbelieving. They *refused* to take up their cross and follow Him.

Our challenge today as modern day "Israelites" is to not repeat their mistake. You and I will never have it as rough as Jesus had it, but Christ tells us there still is a cross we must carry. He knows it's not pleasant, but it leads to the promised land, and He promises to lead the way in the same path He has already trod through twice: Once as the Son of God who led the people of Israel into the promised land, and now as the Son of Man. Jesus knows the way. He is an experienced Guide. Follow Him. Trust Him and you'll arrive safely at your destination.

Five

Joy Over You

The Lord thy God in the midst of thee is mighty; He will save, He will rejoice over thee with joy; He will rest in his love, He will joy over thee with singing (Zephaniah 3:17).

You brought great joy to God on the day you became a Christian. One of my favorite verses in the Bible that I like to share with people is that God joys over us with singing. You can be sure that on the day you gave your life to Christ, all heaven was filled with joy.

But you didn't come to God on your own. It was God that was drawing you and wooing your heart (see Jeremiah 31:3; Revelation 3:20). In the story of the Prodigal Son, it is implied that it was the Spirit of Christ that helped bring the son to his senses. It was the Spirit of Christ that encouraged him to return home. It is no coincidence that in the story the father saw the son while He was yet a great way off. The father was waiting for him.

And he arose, and came to his father. But <u>when he was yet a great way off</u>, his father saw him, and had compassion, and ran, and fell on his neck, and kissed him.

And the son said unto him, Father, I have sinned against heaven, and in thy sight, and am no more worthy to be called thy son.

But the father said to his servants, Bring forth the best robe, and put it on him; and put a ring on his hand, and shoes on his feet:

And bring hither the fatted calf, and kill it; and let us eat, and be merry (Luke 15:20-24).

The story of the Prodigal Son shows us that when God saw you returning home, He ran to you. He ordered your rags be replaced with "the best robe." That robe symbolizes Christ's Robe of Righteousness.

Your joyful welcome home is your assurance of having been accepted in the beloved. Here is another equally stirring passage from the word of God that really helps convey His love and acceptance:

Thus saith the Lord that created thee... Fear not: for I have redeemed thee, I have called thee by thy name; <u>thou art Mine</u>. I am the Lord thy God, the Holy One of Israel, thy Saviour.... Since thou wast precious in My sight, thou hast been honourable, and I have loved thee... Fear not: for I am with thee (Isaiah 43:1,3-5).

This is one of the most touching passages of scripture in the entire Bible. I love it when He says, "thou art Mine." When I read that I always like to say, "yes Lord... yes I am." What a privilege to be loved like that!

So take courage. You are a highly favored child of God. Your present circumstances might betray that thought, but your inheritance is secure.

Remember, we are not home yet. The story of the Prodigal Son shows us that when we started in earnest on our journey toward God, He ran to us and had the best robe put on us. But we are not home yet. When Christ comes again He will take us home and a great feast will be held in our honor, and we will "eat, and be merry."

The Son of God wooed us with His Spirit. The Son of Man paid the penalty for our sins and will someday bring us home. Jesus *will* finish the job. He will bring us home to the Father. Until that day, we need to be patient and wait for His blessed appearing.

Six

ENEMIES AT PEACE

When a man's ways please the Lord, He maketh even his enemies to be at peace with him (Proverbs 16:7).

I learned the truth of this one time with somebody I used to work with years ago. He used to love to give me a hard time and did his best to make my time at work as difficult as possible. On a more civilized occasion, I told him about a really good tofu lasagna recipe that I used to love to make. He could not believe that anything with tofu in it could possibly taste good.

So I got the idea to make him some tofu lasagna to prove my point and brought it to work for him. He heated it up during lunch and absolutely loved it. Much to my surprise, he really liked me after that and couldn't stop talking about my tofu lasagna. That experience taught me the truth of an old saying- "people don't care what you know until they know that you care." I'm sure God was pleased with my actions, and the event proved the truth of Solomon's words- my enemy became at peace with me.

The prophet Elisha was well acquainted with this principle. He had been thwarting the Syrian king's efforts to attack Israel by letting the King of Israel know just where they were going to attack next. Eventually, the King of Syria found out who the source of his trouble was and sent out a great host to capture Elisha. After their arrival, Elisha prayed for the Syrian army to be made blind, and the Lord heard his prayer and struck them with blindness. The prophet then led the army to Samaria. At the prophet's request, their eyes were opened again:

> *And the king of Israel said unto Elisha, when he saw them, My father, shall I smite them? shall I smite them? And he answered, Thou shalt not smite them... set bread and water before them, that they may eat and drink, and go to their master. And he prepared great provision for them: and when they had eaten and drunk, he sent them away, and they went to their master. <u>So the bands of Syria came no more into the land of Israel</u> (2 Kings 6:21-23).*

The king of Syria sent an army to capture Elisha, and what does Elisha do? he feeds them and sends them home. I wish I could have been present to hear the conversation between the returning soldiers and the King of Syria!

So how about you? Is there a nemesis in your life? Remember, Jesus said those who are evil know how to be nice to each other. Our job as Christians is to love the unlovable, to love those who despitefully use us. The Bible says God loved us while we were yet sinners. Now that we have become the children of God, we need to follow God's example and love sinners too.

Loving the saints is easy; loving sinners is divine. So go show your nemesis some love! You never know, you might be surprised to discover your enemy is hurting inside and that things are not the way they might appear to you.

Seven

Prince Of Peace

For unto us a Child is born, unto us a Son is given: and the government shall be upon His shoulder: and His name shall be called Wonderful, Counsellor, The Mighty God, The Everlasting Father, The Prince of Peace (Isaiah 9:6).

We hear this verse a lot during Christmas time, but have you ever thought carefully about what it's saying? This prophecy of the coming Messiah tells us Jesus is the Prince of Peace. That is why the Bible says the meek shall inherit the earth, and shall delight themselves in the abundance of peace (Psalms 37:11). Christ's kingdom will be a kingdom of peace because it will be ruled by the Prince of Peace. What a great promise!

But we don't need to wait until that day to enjoy that peace. We can live in His kingdom now. As a matter of fact, as a child of God it already is yours:

But the Comforter, which is the Holy Ghost, whom the Father will send in My name, He shall teach you all things, and bring all things to your remembrance, whatsoever I have said unto you.

Peace I leave with you, <u>My peace I give unto you</u>: not as the world giveth, give I unto you. Let not your heart be troubled, neither let it be afraid (John 14:26-27).

This peace He promised to give us is the Holy Spirit, the Comforter. But we have a part to play in enjoying that peace. It is impossible to enjoy that peace until we learn to abide with Jesus. We need to put ourselves in an environment where this can happen.

I want to encourage you today to spend time feeding on the word of God. Let it nourish your soul. Make time for prayer. Give Jesus a chance to comfort you and encourage you. Tell Him all about your concerns, and have faith that He will take care of you.

One of the greatest blessings I've discovered over the last year has come from listening to the Bible on YouTube. I had no idea it could be so enjoyable to have someone read the Word of God to you. Maybe you have already discovered that, but if not, you might consider giving it a try sometime. My point is, whether you are in your car, or at home, or wherever you are, take God with you. Take time to read and study His word. Abide with Him and delight yourself in the abundance of peace (Psalms 37:11).

Eight

EXCEEDING YOUR EXPECTATIONS

Able to do exceeding abundantly above all that we ask or think (Ephesians 3:20).

I want to quickly point out here this verse says He is "able" to do exceeding above all that we ask or think. It doesn't say He "will." But with all that in mind, this is still quite a promise. It tells us we serve a mighty God who has no limitations. The only stumbling blocks God has to deal with is the lack of faith in His children. But for those who have faith, all things are possible, to the point of exceeding our expectations. Jesus said:

If ye have faith and doubt not... ye shall say unto this mountain, Be thou removed, and be thou cast into the sea; it shall be done. And all things, whatsoever ye shall ask in prayer, believing, ye shall receive (Matthew 21:21-22).

But we must always ask in accordance with His will. And it is certainly in accordance with His will that all your needs be taken care of.

I have been young, and now am old; yet have I not seen the righteous forsaken, nor his seed begging bread (Psalms 37:25).

The wilderness wanderings of the people of Israel assure us that God will always take care of our needs. God provided them with a cloud by day to shelter them from the hot sun, a pillar of fire by night to keep them warm. He gave them manna from heaven every morning and water out of the rock. The Bible says not even their clothes or their shoes wore out (see Deuteronomy 29:5). By a miracle of divine power, God preserved them. They were able to survive in a desolate wilderness for forty years. We serve a mighty God!

When the people of Israel were down in the valley going about their daily business, Balak the King of Moab tried to get Balaam to pronounce a curse on them. The people were ignorant of the scheming of the enemy, but God was vigilant and on top of the situation and took care of His children. When all was said and done, instead of curses, Balaam wound up pronouncing three blessings on the people of Israel!

You might feel sometimes like God is not doing anything for you, or maybe you think He is not doing enough. But if the curtains could be drawn back and you could see behind the scenes you would see God is still working on your behalf.

The people of Israel had the privilege of seeing far more than we can see with our eyes, but it did nothing to increase their faith, and most of the adults who left Egypt died in the wilderness. They failed just outside the promised land.

Now we are at the end of the world. Once again God's people are on the verge of entering the promised land. I encourage you to not repeat the mistakes of the people who left Egypt. Have faith in God. He *is* able to do far more than you ask or think. Trust Him completely and follow where He leads.

Nine

PEACE WITH GOD

Let him take hold of My strength, that he may make peace with Me; and he shall make peace with Me (Isaiah 27:5).

The "strength" spoken of here refers to salvation through Christ Jesus, because we know that is the only way to have peace with God. The Hebrew writer says it is a fearful thing to fall into the hands of the living God (Hebrews 10:31).

God is unique. He is not just a tender, loving heavenly Father, He is also a Judge. Aren't you glad you made peace with the Judge? What a blessing to have God love us now as one of His dear children. All thanks to the gift of His Son and His sacrifice for our sins.

Another benefit of having been adopted into the household of God is that we now have the "ear" of our heavenly Father:

And it shall come to pass, that <u>before</u> they call, I will answer; and while they are yet speaking, I will hear (Isaiah 65:24).

As you may know, this is often referred to as the "unspoken prayer." The woman with the issue of blood was healed for this very reason. She was a child of God, and God was listening to her heart, even though she did not directly address Him (see Mark 5:25-34). Only the children of God enjoy this privilege. As a child of God, you have the assurance that God is listening to you before you even ask!

Your Father knoweth what things ye have need of, <u>before</u> ye ask Him (Matthew 6:8).

That's why He already knows what you need because He is listening to your heart. As one of His children, He is very interested in what is going on in your life and promises to provide for all of your needs.

As mentioned before, the Bible tells us our prayers are stored in a golden vial (Revelation 5:8). But did you know God also keeps a bottle with your tears?

Thou tellest my wanderings: put Thou my tears into Thy bottle: are they not in Thy book (Psalms 56:8)?

God cares deeply for you. He has the greatest regard for your thoughts, your prayers, and especially your tears. I encourage you to pour out your heart and soul to Him in prayer. Tell Him all about your troubles and your concerns. He is your Friend. He really does want to hear about all the little details in your life. You cannot bore Him or weary Him with your troubles. He loves you too much for that.

God is our refuge and strength, a very present help in trouble (Psalms 46:1).

Ten

Peaceable Habitations

And the work of righteousness shall be peace; and the effect of righteousness quietness and assurance for ever. And My people shall dwell in a peaceable habitation, and in sure dwellings, and in quiet resting places (Isaiah 32:17-18).

Do you realize as a child of God you are the son or daughter of a *multi-zillionaire*? The reward of those who are saved is going to be great. It will defy belief.

But as it is written, Eye hath not seen, nor ear heard, neither have entered into the heart of man, the things which God hath prepared for them that love Him (1 Corinthians 2:9).

Have you ever spent time thinking about what you want? The Bible tells us He is able to do exceeding abundantly above all that we ask or think (Ephesians 3:20). Well let me tell you, I can imagine quite a lot. I'm sure you can too.

I encourage you to spend some time thinking about the after life. It's very comforting. God has told us a little bit about it because He wants us to have something to look forward to. It's meant to cheer us along our journey through this wilderness.

Let me assure you, it will not be like the cartoons I used to watch when I was a kid. I remember when a cartoon character died they would immediately float up to a cloud and start playing the harp. If you have ever been exposed to any of that, I encourage you to pay no mind to it.

The Bible tells us we will have a body like Jesus had after His resurrection (see Luke 24:36-43; Philippians 3:20-21). We will have homes and be able to plant and build and we won't have to worry about someone stealing our things (see Isaiah 32:18; 65:21-22).

> *But the meek shall inherit the earth; and shall delight themselves in the abundance of peace (Psalms 37:1).*

There will be no locks on the doors, no police, no fireman, no doctors and no more tears- and no taxes. We will all be children of God- and Jesus told Peter the children are free from taxation (see Matthew 17:24-26).

I'm sure you've heard the old saying- "there are two things you can count on, death and taxes." In the afterlife, there are also two things you can count on- life and freedom from taxes. Praise God for that! So start your planning- just don't pack your bags yet. God still needs you to let your light shine in this dark world of sin.

Eleven

VIA DOLOROSA

I will instruct thee and teach thee in the way which thou shalt go: I will guide thee with Mine eye (Psalms 32:8).

In Jeremiah 10:23 we learn that it's not in man to direct his steps. And how can we? We are finite and sinful. So thank God He has promised to guide us along the way.

<u>Trust in the Lord with all thine heart</u>; and lean not unto thine own understanding. In all thy ways acknowledge Him, and He shall direct thy paths (Proverbs 3:5-6).

There are three conditions presented in this verse before guidance is given. The first one is that we need to completely trust God.

Second, we need to avoid relying on our own understanding. This requires humbleness of mind. It requires us to recognize our weakness and our need of God. We will never fully understand God and His ways. They will always be a bit of a mystery to us:

For My thoughts are not your thoughts, neither are your ways My ways, saith the Lord.

For as the heavens are higher than the earth, so are My ways higher than your ways, and My thoughts than your thoughts (Isaiah 55:8-9).

And third, we need to always acknowledge God, something Peter failed to do when He denied His Master three times. When these conditions are met, guidance is assured.

And thine ears shall hear a word behind thee, saying, This is the way, walk ye in it, when ye turn to the right hand, and when ye turn to the left (Isaiah 30:21).

One of the smartest things we can ever say as Christians is to 'let the Lord do what seems good to Him' (1 Samuel 3:18; 2 Samuel 10:12). We need to learn to submit ourselves to God's providence and let Him have His own way. We should always try to do everything we can to get out of our bad circumstances. But once we have done everything in our power and nothing changes, we need to recognize that God has ordained in His providence the situation we find ourselves in and submit to it.

This is not always easy to do. But God has provided us with a way to cope with that paradox we all have to deal with from time to time: "How can a God that loves me so much allow so many bad things to happen to me?" The answer to that question is at the cross of Christ.

Whatever you are going through, Jesus has gone through, and then some. And the Father is suffering too. Anyone with children knows how hard it is to watch them suffer.

We must all walk down the *Via Dolorosa* on the way to the promised land. But we are in it together with God, and He will hold us up until we make it home. Our part is to abide in Jesus and to keep following where He leads.

Twelve

PEACE, BE STILL

> *And He arose, and rebuked the wind, and said unto the sea, Peace, be still. And the wind ceased, and there was a great calm (Mark 4:39).*

Moments before Jesus calmed the wind and the sea the disciples were scared and asked Him, "Master, carest thou not that we perish?" Have you ever felt like that? There are times when things can get so bad you can't help but wonder if God really cares.

On that day out on the lake, there is something I want you to see. The disciples crossed the lake at the bidding of *Jesus*.

> *And the same day, when the even was come, He saith unto them, Let us pass over unto the other side (Mark 4:35).*

They were obeying God. They were doing all the right things, and then they got hit by the storm. How sad that must have made Jesus to be asked that question! Jesus did care if they perished, and He cares if you perish as well. Like the disciples, He will bring you through the storm and you will emerge on the other side better and stronger. But will the other side be free of trouble? Let's take a look:

> *And they came over unto the other side of the sea, into the country of the Gadarenes. And when He was come out of the ship, immediately there met Him out of the tombs a man with an unclean spirit, who had his dwelling among the tombs; and no man could bind him, no, not with chains (Mark 5:1-3).*

After a rough night on the lake, the disciples were "welcomed" to the other side by a man with an unclean spirit! The Bible does not tell us how the disciples reacted, but after that terrible night on the lake, their nerves must have been badly shaken. In Luke's account of the story, we learn the man was naked. I suspect that to have this man approach them must have scared them quite a bit.

But Jesus was still with them. Soon the man was "clothed, and in his right mind" (Luke 8:35). And the disciples were O.K. Nothing bad happened to them; just rattled nerves.

All was good. It's always good when Jesus is around. Take Him with you today. He who calmed the wind and the sea and brought the man with an unclean spirit into his right mind can still say, "peace, be still."

Thirteen

Perfect Peace

Thou wilt keep him in perfect peace, whose mind is stayed on Thee: because he trusteth in Thee (Isaiah 26:3).

Jesus told us that in this world we will have tribulation (John 16:33). The promise in this verse from Isaiah is that in spite of that tribulation, if we maintain our trust in Jesus, He will keep us in perfect peace.

Perfect peace is that peace which surpasses all understanding. It's the peace that enabled Jesus to sleep in the boat during the storm out on the lake (see Matthew 8:24-26). This peace went everywhere He went. As we abide in Him, this peace can be ours.

These things I have spoken unto you, that in Me ye might have peace (John 16:33).

If you read the above passage from Isaiah again, you will see it's all about trust. If we trust in Jesus, we will have peace. Peace is the result of total surrender- total and complete *trust* in God.

There was no reason for the disciples to be distressed when they were out in the storm with Jesus. It's a lack of trust in God that brings anxiety and distress. At some point in our Christian experience, we have to learn to completely trust God. We need to surrender ourselves completely into His loving arms and trust Him no matter what. This can be difficult to do.

We have all been hurt by someone. We have all experienced disappointment with others. This can make it hard to trust. But the Bible says, "God is not a man, that He should lie" (Numbers 23:19). And, "God cannot be tempted with evil" (James 1:13). It is impossible for God to treat you badly. Christ's death on the cross is His eternal testimony of His undying love for you. God can always be trusted one-hundred percent.

One of the ways we learn to trust and reverence God is through our earthly father. The fifth commandment says to honor your father and your mother (Exodus 20:12). This is a very important commandment because God knows if you can't honor your earthly father, you will never honor your heavenly Father. The two are linked.

I realize many people grew up in a house where their Dad behaved badly most of the time. Fathers who act like that are doing God a great disservice. They are not modeling godliness. And they are making it more difficult for their children to trust God.

No matter what you have been through, I encourage you to take another chance and trust God completely. Don't hold anything back. Be like Job, who after going through some terrible times was still able to cry out, "though He slay me, yet will I trust in Him" (Job 13:15).

Spend more time praying and reading His word. This will build your trust in Him. Think back also to the times in your life where God has pulled through for you. This will help to increase your faith and trust and enable you to experience that "perfect peace" He wants you to enjoy.

Fourteen

GRACE AND PEACE

Grace to you and peace from God our Father, and the Lord Jesus Christ (Romans 1:7).

Have you ever noticed that most of the letters in the new testament start out that way? When Jesus first saw the disciples after His resurrection, He said, "peace be unto you." This is God's message to you today. It's a message of favor and of peace.

Jesus wants you to experience that abundant life He promised. That's why He came, that you might have life and that you might have it more abundantly (John 10:10).

God is on your side. Whatever mess you are in God can unravel it, no matter how complicated. You are highly favored. God and His holy angels are at your disposal. You can not loose. You have already won because Jesus won at the cross.

The Bible says that while we were yet sinners, Christ died for us (Romans 5:8). This is His grace. It is His unmerited favor- favor we don't deserve. Wonder of wonders! God has shown us mercy- mercy we do not deserve. We are so undeserving of mercy and yet God showed us great mercy in the gift of His Son. Now we are privileged to be among His precious children.

As His adopted children, He wants to give us peace. I experienced that peace when my son got cancer. As I mentioned earlier, He almost died. I cannot begin to tell you about the wonderful peace I had after he came back from his six-hour surgery that almost took his life. I remember I was on my knees praying in the PICU and had my hand over his head. I felt perfectly calm and at peace, and was ready to accept death or life. I remember if my son died, I had already planned to post on Facebook, "the Lord gave, and the Lord hath taken away; blessed be the name of the Lord" (Job 1:21). But for whatever reason, God spared his life and he is now very energetic and full of mischief!

I learned from that experience God will give you the peace you need proportional to the trial you are going through. But I don't want to mislead you. I had been in the middle of a season of prayer and was praying for about five hours a day on my knees for many months before going into that dreadful trial. I had a solid relationship with God, and He bore me in His arms during that time.

Jesus said, "all power is given unto me" (Matthew 28:18). That is the truth. He is powerful and can do anything. He can easily calm the storms of life. Let me assure you, He can also give you that peace which surpasses all understanding. Abide in Him as He asked you to do. Remember, "weeping may endure for a night, but joy cometh in the morning" (Psalms 30:5).

Stay close to Jesus today. In His arms, He will bear you up. Faithful is He who has promised.

Fifteen

FRUITS OF THE SPIRIT

But the fruit of the Spirit is love, joy, peace, longsuffering, gentleness, goodness, faith, meekness, temperance: against such there is no law (Galatians 5:22-23).

It's a sad truth that prosperity does not bring out the best in us. But our growth as Christians is important to God. He wants us to bear fruit and bring honor and glory to His name. It is a law of nature that pruning yields more fruit. So if you are suffering, consider the possibility that you are being pruned by God. It's a painful process, but fruit bearing is what God has in mind.

Remember, God will never waste His time on a useless plant. If you are being pruned, it's because you are valuable and important. It's also important to remember the gardener is always closest to the plant when it is being pruned. It's carefully studied and cut in just the right places.

God is a Master Gardener. He makes no mistakes. He takes no pleasure in trimming your branches. But He has an end goal in mind. He wants you to share in His holiness. He wants you to bear much fruit. God wants to answer His Son's prayer in John chapter seventeen. He wants us all to be united in love.

God wants you to be Christlike. This will happen as you abide in the Vine and bear much fruit. The good news is, heaven can start here on earth. We can live in the atmosphere of heaven as we spend time with the Lord. We can let our light shine and reveal to those around us that the religion of Jesus Christ is for real.

Because of sin, the beauty of God's character has been hidden from those around us. The only way it can be seen is if it is reflected in the lives of Christians. It's the only way the doctrines of the Bible can stand out against those of other religions.

Fruit bearing is a form of evangelism. It's a way we can share the good news of the gospel with those around us. The fruits of the Spirit have a delightful fragrance about them that has the power to attract others to the gospel so that they too can taste and see that the Lord is good.

So friend, let God trim your branches. It's a painful process. But don't ever feel like you are being singled out. Every child of God has to go through it at some point in time. If you hang in there, you will eventually see that the work of the Husbandman will have given way to some really tasty fruit and you will bring honor and glory to His name.

Sixteen

I Will

I will not leave you comfortless: I will come to you (John 14:18).

Pay close attention anytime God says, "I will." When He says that, rest assured it's a done deal. God is not a man that He should lie (Numbers 23:19). He is faithful (Psalms 119:90). And every word of God is pure (Proverbs 30:5).

Moses at one time had some doubts about that. After his fateful encounter with God at the burning bush, God sent Him back to Egypt with a mission- to set the people of Israel free.

As you might recall, Pharaoh was haughty and defiant and refused to let the captives go. He responded by making the burdens of the people of Israel even harder. The people complained to Moses and Moses became very distraught. He went to God and said:

Lord, wherefore hast Thou so evil entreated this people? why is it that Thou hast sent me?

For since I came to Pharaoh to speak in Thy name, he hath done evil to this people; neither hast Thou delivered Thy people at all (Exodus 5:22-23).

Have you ever felt like that? "Lord, what are you doing? why aren't you keeping your promises? don't you care?" Listen now to what God said to Moses:

Wherefore say unto the children of Israel, I am the Lord, and <u>I will</u> bring you out from under the burdens of the Egyptians, and <u>I will</u> rid you out of

> *their bondage, and I will redeem you with a stretched out arm, and with great judgments:*
>
> *And I will take you to Me for a people, and I will be to you a God: and ye shall know that I am the Lord your God, which bringeth you out from under the burdens of the Egyptians.*
>
> *And I will bring you in unto the land, concerning the which I did swear to give it to Abraham, to Isaac, and to Jacob; and I will give it you for an heritage: I am the Lord (Exodus 6:6-8).*

If Pharaoh's knees weren't smacking together one against another in terror when God was saying these words to Moses, they should have been. At the very least his ears should have been ringing. When God says, "I will," the wicked had better watch out! But for the child of God, it is always an assurance of favor.

Rest assured God knows what is happening in your life. His promise to you is, "I will not leave you comfortless: I will come to you" (John 14:18).

Seventeen

Finding Rest

Come unto Me, all ye that labour and are heavy laden, and I will give you rest. Take My yoke upon you, and learn of Me; for I am meek and lowly in heart: and ye shall find rest unto your souls. For My yoke is easy, and My burden is light (Matthew 11:28-30).

"Come unto me... and I will give you rest." This rest is found in prayer. It's also found in His word. But there is nothing quite like finding it in prayer. Jesus is full of peace. Spending time with Him brings peace.

I have found great peace on my knees in prayer. You can too. This peace that is found in Jesus is what makes our yoke easy and our burden light. Sometimes we are so busy we forget to take a "vacation" with Jesus. There are times in our lives when we need to have special seasons of prayer- of abiding with Jesus:

And He said unto them, Come ye yourselves apart into a desert place, and rest a while: for there were many coming and going, and they had no leisure so much as to eat (Mark 6:31).

Jesus sensed the disciples needed a break. Maybe that is where you are. Maybe it's time to head out to the desert. That is where Jesus took the disciples. I suspect the desert here represents what many refer to as the "prayer closet." It's a quiet, uninhabited place where you can go to spend some quality time with God.

The desert is also a fitting symbol for life on earth. After all, that is where God took the people of Israel after they came out of Egypt. He took them into an uninhabited wilderness, to spend some time with Him, to help them grow in faith before bringing them into the promised land.

Pharaoh had the people of Israel so busy they didn't have time to do much of anything but work. I'm sure it hasn't escaped your notice that most people around you are rushing here and there- frantically trying to pack in as much as possible into the day. Let me assure you, this is the spiritual equivalent of Pharaoh and his taskmasters playing the role of slave drivers. Little to no time to pray and read the Bible- just work, work, work. This is Pharaoh's message for you today:

> *Ye are idle, ye are idle: therefore ye say, Let us go and do sacrifice to the Lord. Go therefore now, and work; for there shall no straw be given you, yet shall ye deliver the tale of bricks (Exodus 5:17-18).*

God's message is:

> *Come ye yourselves apart into a desert place, and rest a while (Mark 6:31).*

I want to encourage you to make time for the Lord. Don't let "Pharaoh" keep you busy gathering straw and making bricks to build up his kingdom. Cooperate with God in building up *His* kingdom, a kingdom that will have no end (Luke 1:33).

Never forget, you are better off in the desert with Jesus than in Egypt with Pharaoh. It's my prayer today you will flee from the "taskmasters" and enjoy rest in the desert with our "meek and lowly" Friend.

Eighteen

FREEDOM FROM FEAR

But whoso hearkeneth unto Me shall dwell safely, and shall be quiet from fear of evil (Proverbs 1:33).

We are told in the last days men's hearts would be failing them for fear (Luke 21:26). But this does not have to be a problem for the child of God:

God hath not given us the spirit of fear; but of power, and of love, and of a sound mind (2 Timothy 1:7).

We live in difficult times. Everything in the world seems so unstable. Things you used to be able to count on just aren't there anymore. For instance, you can be gainfully employed one day, and unemployed the next. There also seems to be a fine line of civility between people that can easily be broken when a crisis arises.

I lived in the Washington, DC metro area for many years. I remember sometime around the turn of the millennium there was a snow storm that hit the area just hours before it was time for everyone to get off work. Traffic was a nightmare. I lived just a few miles from my work and I remember it took about two hours of "driving" to get home. This in itself was fairly uneventful except for one thing. People were running red lights like nothing I had ever seen before. That is what made traffic so bad. I remember when I got home and watched the news, one of the news anchors complained about it and called the red light running for what it was- "lawlessness." That's when I realized it was happening all over the metro area.

I'm sure you can probably think of a few examples of your own. Most of the people around us are not grounded on the solid Rock we know to symbolize Jesus Christ. But we have the assurance as Christians that we need not be afraid. While others are panicking in fear to get home from the "snowstorms" of life, we can remain calm and at peace.

> *Yea, though I walk through the valley of the shadow of death, I will fear no evil: for Thou art with me; Thy rod and Thy staff they comfort me (Psalms 23:4).*

No matter where you are in your life, I hope and pray you will trust in God to provide for you. Many years ago I learned that worry is actually a sin. Did you know we bring dishonor to God when we fret and worry like an unbeliever? We have a mighty God to take care of us. Besides, worry does not accomplish anything.

We do need to work out our problems and try to solve them as best we can, but once we have done everything in our power to fix things, we need to leave the rest with God. Trust in God and don't sin by worrying. And remember what Jesus said:

> *Take therefore no thought for the morrow: for the morrow shall take thought for the things of itself. Sufficient unto the day is the evil thereof (Matthew 6:34).*

Nineteen

THOUGHTS OF PEACE

For I know the thoughts that I think toward you, saith the Lord, thoughts of peace, and not of evil, to give you an expected end (Jeremiah 29:11).

There are times in our lives when it's hard to believe that God is our friend, let alone our loving heavenly Father. Trouble after trouble comes our way that tests our faith to the utmost.

Hannah once found herself in that very situation. Her husband Elkanah had another wife by the name of Peninnah. The Bible tells us Peninnah had sons and daughters, but Hannah had no children.

And her adversary also provoked her sore, for to make her fret, because the Lord had shut up her womb. And as he did so year by year, when she went up to the house of the Lord, so she provoked her; therefore she wept, and did not eat (1 Samuel 1:6-7).

Anyone who has ever had a nemesis to contend with can sympathize with this woman's situation. But Hannah was a child of God. She knew just what to do. She went to the temple and poured out her soul to God in prayer:

And she was in bitterness of soul, and prayed unto the Lord, and wept sore. And she vowed a vow, and said, O Lord of hosts, if Thou wilt indeed look on the affliction of Thine handmaid, and remember me, and not forget Thine handmaid, but wilt give unto Thine handmaid a man child, then I will give him unto the Lord all the days of his life, and there shall no razor come upon his head (1 Samuel 1:10-11).

Because Hannah's lips moved while she was quietly praying, Eli the High Priest mistook her for a drunk:

> *And Hannah answered and said, No, my lord, I am a woman of a sorrowful spirit: I have drunk neither wine nor strong drink, but have poured out my soul before the Lord... for out of the abundance of my complaint and grief have I spoken hitherto. Then Eli answered and said, Go in peace: and the God of Israel grant thee thy petition that thou hast asked of Him. So the woman went her way, and did eat, and her countenance was no more sad (1 Samuel 1:15-18).*

God answered her prayer, and shortly after she gave birth to Samuel, who would go on to become one of the greatest of God's prophets. As the story of Hannah shows us, adversity and grinding trials are the seed God uses to give birth to future blessings.

Our verse from Jeremiah tells us God has thoughts of peace towards you, and not of evil. Won't you follow Hannah's example and take your problems to God? Pour out your soul before the Lord. You are one of His precious children. Give Him the opportunity to comfort you and help you.

Twenty

I Can Do All Things

I can do all things through Christ which strengtheneth me (Philippians 4:13).

There are days when it's hard to get out of bed. Days when death seems preferable to life. Two of the giants of the Bible had such days.

Whence should I have flesh to give unto all this people? for they weep unto me, saying, Give us flesh, that we may eat. I am not able to bear all this people alone, because it is too heavy for me. And if Thou deal thus with me, kill me, I pray Thee, out of hand, if I have found favour in Thy sight; and let me not see my wretchedness (Numbers 11:13-15).

Poor Moses. He was definitely having a bad day! Take a look now at Elijah after he fled from Jezebel who had threatened to kill him:

But he himself went a day's journey into the wilderness, and came and sat down under a juniper tree: and he requested for himself that he might die; and said, It is enough; now, O Lord, take away my life; for I am not better than my fathers (1 Kings 19:4).

But God was not interested in taking their life. He gave them something far better. He strengthened them. And where are they now? The Bible tells us they are in heaven. They were also the two individuals who had the honor of appearing with Jesus at the Mount of Transfiguration (see Matthew 17:1-8).

Job had it much worse that Moses or Elijah. He lost everything he had, including his health, and also took to despairing of life.

After this opened Job his mouth, and cursed his day. And Job spake, and said, Let the day perish wherein I was born, and the night in which it was said, There is a man child conceived. Why died I not from the womb? why did I not give up the ghost when I came out of the belly?(Job 3:1-3,11).

A few verses later he made some really interesting comments:

Wherefore is light given to him that is in misery, and life unto the bitter in soul; which long for death, but it cometh not; and dig for it more than for hid treasures; which rejoice exceedingly, and are glad, when they can find the grave? Why is light given to a man whose way is hid, and whom God hath hedged in (Job 3:20-23)?

That is some serious agony of mind and spirit! And yet when you compare the first chapter of Job with the last chapter of the book, you can see God restored to him double what he had before the crisis hit (see 1:2-3; 42:12-13).

Job had ten children before he lost them through the crisis, and ten children were born to him after crisis. You might be wondering how that makes for double. But remember, those children are saved. He had ten to start and twenty at the end! Job really did have *double* restored to him.

Like Job, God promises to give you an expected end of peace (Jeremiah 29:11). For now, He wants you to trust in Him. Abide in Him and let Him strengthen you.

Know that God is with you. He will help you and hold you up. He loves you and knows all about your troubles. He can unravel them and give you the strength you need to bear your trials with grace.

Twenty-one

WAIT ON THE LORD

But they that wait upon the Lord shall renew their strength; they shall mount up with wings as eagles; they shall run, and not be weary; and they shall walk, and not faint (Isaiah 40:31).

Are you feeling tired and weak to the point of fainting? This verse is a great promise for those who are struggling to get out of bed in the morning. But what does it mean to *wait* on the Lord?

I remember when I first became a Christian I was thirty pounds overweight. I had a terrible diet, didn't exercise, and had a rotten attitude. Within ten weeks of my conversion, I lost thirty pounds, was running five miles a day, was eating healthy meals, and had a completely different outlook on life. My attitude changed 180 degrees. How did that happen? I *waited* on the Lord.

The Hebrew word for "wait" in the above passage from Isaiah is "Qavah." It means to wait, to look for, or to bind together, perhaps in a twisting like manner. What this means is that there is incredible power at your disposal, but you must first bind yourself to God before you can tap into that power.

If ye abide in Me, and My words abide in you, ye shall ask what ye will, and it shall be done unto you (John 15:7).

We abide when we spend time reading His word, and especially when we spend time in prayer. Prayer is the key to abiding. Disciplining ourselves to spend much time in prayer every day is how we bind ourselves to God. That is what waiting on Him is all about. The importance of prayer is a recurring theme in my books because I know from experience what happens when you spend a lot of time in prayer.

When you pray, you are hooking up to the most incredible power source in the universe. Our sun is nothing compared to God. There is *nothing* mightier than God. God wants you to be strong. It is your privilege. It is your divine right as one of God's children.

> *Wait on the Lord: be of good courage, and He shall strengthen thine heart: wait, I say, on the Lord (Psalms 27:14).*

That is not accomplished by spending a few minutes in prayer before going to bed at the end of the day. I'm talking about establishing new priorities where prayer becomes the most important part of your life. There are twenty-four hours in a day. Let me assure you if you manage your time carefully, and change your priorities there is room for spending *more time* with God.

When Jesus Christ comes back in the clouds of heaven with power and great glory, those who learn to *wait* on the Lord through prayer will one day exclaim:

> *Lo, this is our God; we have waited for Him, and He will save us: this is the Lord; we have waited for Him, we will be glad and rejoice in His salvation (Isaiah 25:9).*

Twenty-two

Wonderfully Made

> *And the Lord God formed man of the dust of the ground, and breathed into his nostrils the breath of life; and man became a living soul (Genesis 2:7).*

Have you ever tried to figure out why God loves you so much? Job found himself wondering that at one time.

> *What is man, that thou shouldest magnify him? and that thou shouldest set thine heart upon him (Job 7:17)?*

It is a bit of a mystery at times, even for those of us who are parents. Being a parent does give a lot of insight into the mind of God, but I've learned that is not the only way to better understand Him. We also learn to understand Him when we make and create things ourselves.

I don't know about you, but when I make an effort at building or creating something, I care about it. The more effort I put into it, the more I care. If something were to come along and destroy it, I would not be happy. And all I can ever make are inanimate objects that will never return any love to me.

So by making things, that is certainly one of the ways we can learn why God cares about us so much. The Bible tells us He *formed* the birds of the air and the beasts of the field from the ground (Genesis 2:19). Jesus said not even a sparrow falls to the ground without

God taking notice, and He assured us we are more valuable than many sparrows (Matthew 10:29,31).

God put thought, time, and effort into creating this planet. How much time He spent in the planning phase the Bible does not tell us, but we are privileged to know it took six days worth of work. God could have snapped His fingers and it all would have appeared instantly, but He chose to take His time.

Man is the crowning act of creation. The scriptures tell us God *formed* man from the dust of the ground (Genesis 2:7). That He took His time in carefully forming man with His own hands shows there was a lot of love put into the effort. Then those same lips that would one day cry out, "it is finished," breathed in man the breath of life. At the end of the six days He looked at His creation and saw that it was "very good" (Genesis 1:31).

The Bible says you are "fearfully and wonderfully made" (Psalms 139:14). God loves humanity so much, He provides even for those who hate Him. They also enjoy the sunshine, air, gravity, food, and water that God provides. Think about that for a minute. God cares about His entire creation- even people who *hate* Him.

When you think about God's love and the effort He made at creating us; how He works to maintain life on this planet; the gift of His only Son; how He cares even for those who hate him- it must grieve His heart terribly when *His own children* don't trust Him.

Friend, won't you resolve today to trust God one-hundred percent? Resolve not to grieve His tender heart anymore. God is trustworthy. He cares about you. He will take care of all of your needs and make everything in your life work for the good. He promises to also give you peace of mind if you abide in Him.

Twenty-three

IS ANYTHING TOO HARD FOR ME?

Behold, I am the Lord, the God of all flesh: is there any thing too hard for Me (Jeremiah 32:27)?

It's amazing to read that Nicodemus, who was a Pharisee and a ruler of Israel, was clueless about the new birth experience:

Jesus answered and said unto him, Verily, verily, I say unto thee, Except a man be born again, he cannot see the kingdom of God. Nicodemus saith unto Him, How can a man be born when he is old? can he enter the second time into his mother's womb, and be born (John 3:3-4)?

We have a lot more information about God than Nicodemus ever dreamed possible. We are a privileged generation. We have the entire Word of God at our disposal. It contains an incredible amount of information about Him. Faith in God should not be a problem for us.

It does not matter what you are going through today, God can fix it. That is His specialty. Our only job is to trust in Him and let Him fix it in His own time and way.

As any seasoned Christian will tell you, God is notorious for taking His time in fixing the problem. He does not do that to torment us, though. It pains Him deeply to see us in distress. But God has a higher good in mind. He wants us to grow in character.

Unfortunately, prosperity does not promote character growth. As a matter of fact, it tends to have the opposite effect. But God's promise is to be with you through your trials. He will help you. He always does:

> *Is my hand shortened at all, that it cannot redeem? or have I no power to deliver (Isaiah 50:2)?*

You might think your problems exceed anything God can fix. But let me assure you, God *can* still make some tasty lemonade out of your lemons. But it takes time. This requires patience.

> *For with God nothing shall be impossible (Luke 1:37).*

The same powerful God that spoke the earth into existence, that raised the dead, that healed the sick is at your disposal today. He can do anything, and your problems are not beyond anything He can handle.

Twenty-four

PEACEMAKERS

Blessed are the peacemakers: for they shall be called the children of God (Matthew 5:9).

This is a wonderful promise we can claim and take action on right away. You don't have to be an ambassador for your country to do this. As God's ambassador, you can apply this right at home or at work.

Whenever I used to see people at the office who were not getting along too well, I would try to get one of them to say something positive about their nemesis. Then when the opportunity would arise, I would go and repeat that positive comment to the other person they weren't getting along with. I'd keep repeating that process back and forth until things got smoothed over. That's what you call building bridges! That's doing the Lord's work, and it's something you can easily do today.

The power of words to sooth was a principle Gideon put into practice on one occasion. After he routed the enemy with the help of the Lord, the people of Ephraim were quite upset with him for not having initially asked them for help:

And the men of Ephraim said unto him, Why hast thou served us thus, that thou calledst us not, when thou wentest to fight with the Midianites? And they did chide with him sharply.

And he said unto them, What have I done now in comparison of you? Is not the gleaning of the grapes of Ephraim better than the vintage of Abiezer?

God hath delivered into your hands the princes of Midian, Oreb and Zeeb: and what was I able to do in comparison of you? Then their anger was abated toward him, when he had said that (Judges 8:1-3).

There is another good reason to be a peacemaker and build bridges. I've learned one of the best ways to get your mind off of your troubles is to focus on the needs of those around you. There are a lot of people in pain all around us. They are hurting inside and in many cases angry at someone or something. They are waiting for words of encouragement from you- God's Ambassador.

Blessed are the peacemakers. I encourage you to claim this blessing from God and be a peacemaker today.

Twenty-five

PRAYER THAT AVAILS MUCH

The effectual fervent prayer of a righteous man availeth much (James 5:16).

Jesus already promised to provide you with everything you need. He has assured you that all you need is to seek first the kingdom of God and his righteousness and all those things would already be yours (Matthew 6:33).

So what is the best use we can make of this promise? I believe we need to focus on others, especially those who are lost. This promise is our assurance that God will send His holy angels to go to the aid of our loved ones who are not walking with the Lord.

If your heart aches for them, James 5:16 is your assurance that God will send them help. Let me assure you, there is *nothing* more "effectual" in God's eyes than praying for the lost! Jesus died on the cross so they could be saved. He cares deeply for those around us, including our loved ones that we earnestly pray for.

Through the prayer of faith, God will send His holy angels to go and minister to His wayward children. Their influence is very subtle and gentle, but rest assured they are there.

Because of the subtle nature of this process, it can take a lot of time before you see any results. Engaging in this type of work requires a strong determination on our part. In most cases this will prove to be a long, protracted warfare. This type of warfare will test the "metal" of the prayer warrior to the utmost.

But as a Christian, you are wearing Christ's Breastplate of Righteousness. That "metal" has already been tried in the furnace of affliction and proven itself. So the love of Christ in our hearts will drive us to keep praying until the day God calls us to lay our armor down.

We have the assurance in the scriptures that even after we die, God will not forget our prayers for our loved ones. The Bible tells us they are stored in a golden vial.

> *And when He had taken the book, the four beasts and four and twenty elders fell down before the Lamb, having every one of them harps, and <u>golden vials full of odours, which are the prayers of saints</u> (Revelation 5:8).*

The Bible says, "precious in the sight of the Lord is the death of His saints" (Psalms 116:15). This means your prayers in that golden vial become even more precious to Him after you are gone. So keep praying for your loved ones. Do not loose heart.

I know personally of one instance where someone died and many years later her wayward son came back to the Lord. It happens. Don't ever give up. Keep God's holy angels busy! They don't mind it at all. Their hearts are full of love and they are more than eager to help your loved ones.

Twenty-six

I Have Loved You

Since thou wast precious in My sight, thou hast been honourable, and I have loved thee (Isaiah 43:4).

"I have loved thee." Coming from the lips of a holy God that cannot lie or sin makes this statement priceless! Can there be a better assurance of divine favor than that? But did you notice He said, "have *loved* thee." There are quite a few instances in the Bible where God says that in the past tense. Take a look:

- *For God so loved the world (John 3:16).*
- *I have loved you (John 15:12).*
- *The Lord loved you (Deuteronomy 7:8).*
- *The Lord thy God loved thee (Deuteronomy 23:5).*
- *God, who is rich in mercy, for His great love wherewith He loved us (Ephesians 2:4).*

This verse gives us a pretty good idea why He keeps talking to us that way:

The Lord hath appeared of old unto me, saying, Yea, <u>I have loved thee with an everlasting love</u>: therefore with lovingkindness have I drawn thee (Jeremiah 31:3).

So God has loved us with an everlasting love! If you are not convinced yet that God loves you deeply, and that He has loved you for a long time, take a look at this verse:

> *How precious also are <u>Thy thoughts unto me, O God!</u> how great is the sum of them! <u>If I should count them, they are **more** in number than the sand</u>: when I awake, I am still with Thee (Psalms 139:17-18).*

God's thoughts towards you are *more* in number than the sand! Obviously, God has been thinking about you to a point so far back in time it defies human comprehension. I think it's pretty safe to say He has you on His mind right now. God has always known about you. Look what He said to Jeremiah:

> *Before I formed thee in the belly I knew thee (Jeremiah 1:5).*

God knows every detail about you. The Bible says even the hairs of your head are numbered:

> *Are not two sparrows sold for a farthing? and one of them shall not fall on the ground without your Father. But <u>the very hairs of your head are all numbered</u>. Fear ye not therefore, ye are of more value than many sparrows. (Matthew 10:29-31).*

But nowhere in the Bible does God say, "I love you" more that when Jesus died on the cross. Friend, God, really does love you. Your circumstances might be absolutely terrible. You might be wondering, "how can a loving God allow so much pain and suffering?" As I've mentioned before, look to the cross. Look to Jesus. The answer to *everything* is at the cross of Christ. Jesus knows all about pain and suffering.

Only when Jesus comes back again will this nightmare be over. Then and only then will we be free of trouble. Until then, God promises to be with you. He has promised to give you the grace and strength to bear your trials with grace. This is the promise of love.

Twenty-seven

PRESERVE YOUR SOUL

The Lord shall preserve thee from all evil: He shall preserve thy soul. The Lord shall preserve thy going out and thy coming in from this time forth, and even for evermore (Psalms 121:7-8).

The wilderness wanderings of the people of Israel after they came out of Egypt show us that God's ways lead through a desert. But no matter where we go in this world of sin, our promise from Psalms 121 is that God will preserve us.

In spite of this assurance, He will allow tests and trials to come our way. I've heard it said, "you are either in a crisis, have just come out of one, or are headed into one." Either way, Jesus was right when He said, "in the world ye shall have tribulation" (John 16:33).

Trouble is the lot of saint and sinner. But as saints, we have assurance the sinner does not have. We have a loving God who promises to be with us every step of the way through this wilderness journey. And He promises to make everything work together for the good (Romans 8:28).

Jesus has walked the streets of planet earth. He has dealt with the same people we have to deal with. He was reproached, mocked, falsely accused, and even betrayed by one of His own friends. Jesus knows this place well. Have you ever been whipped? spat upon? unjustly condemned? killed? Jesus has gone way beyond anything most of us will ever experience.

Jesus is an expert when it comes to life on planet earth. He is an *expert* on suffering. That is why He is able to comfort us. Abide in Him and let Him comfort you. God comforted Him when He walked this earth. Let the Shepherd of your soul comfort you now.

> *Yea, though I walk through the valley of the shadow of death, I will fear no evil: for Thou art with me; Thy rod and Thy staff they comfort me (Psalms 23:4).*

The rod and staff of the Shepherd is symbolic of the judgement and power of God that works in your favor. It was that same rod that brought the plagues on the Egyptians. And it was that same rod that parted the red sea for God's people. So be comforted by the Shepherd's rod. You are the apple of God's eye (Zechariah 2:8). And God says, "I will contend with him that contendeth with thee" (Isaiah 49:25). The judgement of God in your favor might seem delayed, but God promises that it will come.

Twenty-eight

ALL NEEDS SUPPLIED

> *My God shall supply all your need according to His riches in glory by Christ Jesus (Philippians 4:19).*

God's history with His people is one of being a provider. No wonder we are told to refer to Him as our heavenly *Father*. As our Father, He has promised to take care of all of our needs.

In the Bible, a person becomes an adult and are accountable to God when they turn twenty years of age (see Numbers 1:2-3; 14:29,31). As everyone knows, the job of a parent is to train their children to fend for themselves. But that is not how it works with God.

We will always be God's *children*. He will always have to take care of us. And why is that? Because apart from Him, there is no life. All things consist by Him (Colossians 1:17). There is no air, no gravity, no food, no water, no sunshine, no *anything* without Him. We will always be dependent on Him for these things. And so we will be His *children* throughout eternity.

God is well aware of our dependency on Him. He has used the paternal terms of "Father" and "children" to help us better understand our relationship to Him. He does not want us to fret or worry. He has promised to take care of all of our needs. Remember what Jesus said?

> *Take no thought for your life, what ye shall eat, or what ye shall drink; nor yet for your body, what ye shall put on. Behold the fowls of the air: for*

they sow not, neither do they reap, nor gather into barns; yet your heavenly Father feedeth them. Are ye not much better than they? But seek ye first the kingdom of God, and His righteousness; and all these things shall be added unto you (Matthew 6:25-26,33).

As a "child" of God you are already doing that, so don't worry. God promises to take care of you.

Can a woman forget her sucking child, that she should not have compassion on the son of her womb? yea, they may forget, yet will I not forget thee. Behold, I have graven thee upon the palms of My hands; thy walls are continually before Me (Isaiah 49:15-16).

The promise to care for you and provide for all of your needs has been signed and ratified not with ink and pen but with the blood of Christ. It was a part of your "adoption papers" when you were brought into the family of God. It contains your assurance that your heavenly Father will not fail you! Here it is again for those who may have missed it:

What shall we then say to these things? If God be for us, who can be against us? He that spared not His own Son, but delivered Him up for us all, how shall He not with Him also freely give us all things (Romans 8:31-32)?

Twenty-nine

THE COMFORTER

I will pray the Father, and He shall give you another Comforter, that He may abide with you for ever (John 14:16).

Jesus promised to send the Holy Spirit to the disciples after His return to the Father. He referred to the Spirit as the Comforter.

As a child of God, this Comforter is in you and will never leave you. He will abide with you *forever*. Some of these promises are so incredible, they almost take your breath away. *Forever* is a long time!

God's love for us is so deep, He uses the metaphor of a mother comforting her child to help us better understand what He wants to do when we are hurting.

As one whom his mother comforteth, so will I comfort you (Isaiah 66:13).

When you feel discouraged or depressed, go to Jesus. Tell Him about your pain and ask Him to comfort you- to wrap His arms around you. Reverently remind Him of His promise and ask Him to fulfill His word. His word is golden. Abide in Him and let Him comfort you.

It's amazing what God can do. You enter into prayer discouraged and come out feeling peaceful and encouraged. Jesus can still quiet the storms of life. He can still say, "peace, be still." He has a wonderful way of banishing the stormy clouds that can gather around our mind.

You may have heard the old saying, "the soul would have no rainbow had the eyes no tears." Our tears will lead us someday to that rainbow around God's throne (Revelation 4:3). That rainbow symbolizes the power and authority behind the throne of God. It is symbolic of a holy God; a God that is a covenant keeper. It is our assurance that God will do as He said.

God gave us the rainbow when He promised to never flood the earth again (see Genesis 9:8-17). We can all testify that God has kept His promise. Now His promise is that He will come again and take us home to Himself.

> *In My Father's house are many mansions... I go to prepare a place for you.*
>
> *And if I go and prepare a place for you, I will come again, and receive you unto Myself; that where I am, there ye may be also (John 14:2-3).*

The apostle Paul assures us when that day comes that...

> *The Lord Himself shall descend from heaven with a shout, with the voice of the archangel, and with the trump of God: and the dead in Christ shall rise first:*
>
> *Then we which are alive and remain shall be caught up together with them in the clouds, to meet the Lord in the air: and so shall we ever be with the Lord.*
>
> *Wherefore comfort one another with these words (1 Thessalonians 4:16-18).*

Thirty

GOD OF ALL COMFORT

Blessed be God, even the Father of our Lord Jesus Christ, the Father of mercies, and the God of all comfort; Who comforteth us in all our tribulation, that we may be able to comfort them which are in any trouble, by the comfort wherewith we ourselves are comforted of God (2 Corinthians 1:3-4).

I really like the part where God promises to comfort us in *all* our tribulation. *All* is a broad word that encompasses much! God is really going out of His way to let us know we are greatly favored, and that He will always help us out.

Our verse from Corinthians also shows us that one of the benefits of being comforted by God is that it enables us to also follow His example and be a source of comfort to others. The act of comforting has everything to do with mercy and compassion, and mercy and compassion is at the heart of what God is all about.

The apostle Paul called our life on this earth a light affliction which lasts for a moment. If you are like me, you have had some real tough days on this planet. It's hard to think of them as a light momentary affliction. But as hard as it might be for us to buy into that, it's coming from the lips of the apostle Paul, a man who definitely knew a thing or two about suffering:

Of the Jews five times received I forty stripes save one.

Thrice was I beaten with rods, once was I stoned, thrice I suffered shipwreck, a night and a day I have been in the deep;

> *In journeyings often, in perils of waters, in perils of robbers, in perils by mine own countrymen, in perils by the heathen, in perils in the city, in perils in the wilderness, in perils in the sea, in perils among false brethren;*
>
> *In weariness and painfulness, in watchings often, in hunger and thirst, in fastings often, in cold and nakedness.*
>
> *Beside those things that are without, that which cometh upon me daily, the care of all the churches (2 Corinthians 11:24-28).*

It's amazing that after all he had gone through he could say:

> *For our light affliction, which is but for a moment, worketh for us a far more exceeding and eternal weight of glory;*
>
> *While we look not at the things which are seen, but at the things which are not seen: for the things which are seen are temporal; but the things which are not seen are eternal (2 Corinthians 4:17-18).*

It's my prayer today that by faith you will weigh your affliction against the eternal weight of glory that awaits you. And that like the apostle Paul you also look to those "things which are not seen." And always remember- no matter what you are going through:

> *Weeping may endure for a night, but joy cometh in the morning (Psalms 30:5).*

Thirty-one

ALL THINGS NEW

And He that sat upon the throne said, Behold, I make all things new. And He said unto me, Write: for these words are true and faithful (Revelation 21:5).

Speaking of the new earth, in the above passage we learn that God promises to make all things new. Think about this carefully. He said all things *new*- not all new things. God already knows you love the mountains, the fields, and lakes. He knows you love gardens and parks and the blue sky and the green grass and the tall trees and beautiful flowers.

We all love the things of nature. God knows they bring peace. And peace is what the afterlife is all about.

My people shall dwell in a peaceable habitation, and in sure dwellings, and in quiet resting places (Isaiah 32:18).

At the end of the third, fourth, and fifth day of creation the Bible says, "and God saw that it was good." At the end of the sixth day, after creating man we read:

*And <u>God saw everything that</u> He had made, and, behold, **it was very good**. And the evening and the morning were the sixth day (Genesis 1:31).*

After creating man God was very pleased with His whole creation. That is why He is making all things new, and not all new things. It's all the good things without the taint of sin.

> *And I saw a new heaven and a new earth: for the first heaven and the first earth were passed away; and <u>there was no more sea</u> (Revelation 21:1).*

As we can see from the above verse, the only exception will be "no more sea." I take that to mean the vast oceans on this planet will be no more. But I suspect there will be lakes with sandy beaches for us to enjoy. The earth will someday be restored to an Eden-like state of perfection. And you can be sure when that happens we will cry out with the Lord that it all looks "very good." It will be wonderful. Sin and sinners will be no more. No more pain, no more tears. We will get to delight ourselves in the abundance of peace.

> *And God shall wipe away all tears from their eyes; and there shall be no more death, neither sorrow, nor crying, neither shall there be any more pain: for the former things are passed away (Revelation 21:4).*

So hang in there- just a little longer. The night is almost over. In the mean time let us "wait on the Lord" and join in with God's people as we together "look for new heavens and a new earth, wherein dwelleth righteousness" (2 Peter 3:13).

Benediction

The Lord bless thee, and keep thee: The Lord make His face shine upon thee, and be gracious unto thee: The Lord lift up His countenance upon thee, and give thee peace (Numbers 6:24-26).

Made in the USA
Middletown, DE
20 January 2017